Copenhagen. The

Denmark's capital stands a
the trends making the north

From architecture and sustainability to the vegetable-focussed cuisine conquering the world's tables, this community of just half a million people continues to punch above its weight.

And it's all there to enjoy amid a utopic setting of modernist buildings, bike-friendly streets and a harbour clean enough to dive into. The Danes have made an art out of "hygge"—their particular kind of warmth and cosiness.

Sharing their side to Copenhagen are a few local legends: a popular food blogger, an artist couple pushing for analogue life, the frontman of a leading experimental band, a rebellious fashion designer and a pioneer of the Meatpacking District. A feature piece presents childhood in Christiania, a short story takes on Noma and Nordic-noir, and a photo showcase peeks behind the city's shiny façade. It's all about original minds and the creative vibe. Get lost in the sights, sounds and flavours of the city. Get lost in Copenhagen.

Photo: Cirkelbroen, VisitDenmark

Story

Showcase

Icon of Danish modernist architecture and trailblazing furniture designer Arne Jacobsen built the Skovshoved Petrol Station in 1938. And besides the addition of new pumps, it hasn't been altered since. Just north of Copenhagen on the Danish Riviera, motorists can fill up their cars at "The Mushroom" while pondering a spectacular sea view.

• Skovshoved Petrol Station, Kystvejen 24, Charlottenlund

Culture **Fundamental Research**

Danish design is all about simplicity. And it all started in the 19th century with Gustav Friedrich Hetsch's proposal that "aesthetics must always follow function". Using leather, wood and granite, Danes defined taste in the 20th century, with Arne Jacobsen and Hans J. Wegner among the first wave. In the 1960s Verner Panton's playful furniture set another accent. When in 1978 Jacob Jensen's Bang & Olufsen audio products were displayed at New York's MOMA, the world took note. Follow the full story in one of Copenhagen's finest rococo buildings.
• Designmuseum Danmark, Bredgade 68, Indre By, designmuseum.dk

From Sleek Fashion to State-funded Clubbing

Great Danes

Food **Finely Tuned Dining**

Dining behemoth Noma has provided a platform for most of the city's culinary heroes. Its co-founder Claus Meyer teamed up with former sous-chef Jesper Kirketerp to create an informal fine dining option at *Radio*. Next to the city's old radio house, this stylish, woody restaurant owns land and works with local farmers and providers. Ingredients are creatively combined in affordable three or five-course meals. Opt for a wine course or a non-alcoholic drinks menu that will change your conception of "juice".
• Radio, Julius Thomsens Gade 12, Nørrebro, restaurantradio.dk

Outdoors

Architectural Time Travel

Take a break from sleek modernism and vegetable-focussed cuisine to clap your eyes on something anathema to both: the baroque masterpiece of the *Hermitage Hunting Lodge* (pictured). Built in the 1730s for King Christian VI to host banquets, it still provides the setting for royal lunches and can be entered with advance booking Jun 1–Aug 31. The tour is in Danish. Even outside these dates the setting of the building, overlooking the Øresund coast and surrounded by plains often filled with deer, is breathtaking. A short drive away—or near Klampenborg train station—is *Bellevue Beach*, where you can return to white cubes with one of Arne Jacobsen's first projects. The Danish architect was a believer in "Gesamtkunstwerk", or the total work of art. So he designed everything at Bellevue, from the watchtowers to staff uniforms and entry tickets. There too is Jacobsen's *Bellevue Theatre*, with a roof that retracts for summer performances.

• Hermitage Hunting Lodge, Lyngby; Bellevue Beach and Theatre, Klampenborg

Outdoors **Soakenhagen**

Copenhagen summers might be shorter than the Mediterranean, but jumping in the water is just as appealing. Luckily the city offers plenty of choices to show off your new swim wear, and, if you choose, your birthday suit. The selection ranges from lively harbour bath *Islands Brygge* (Amager) or the quieter olympic sized pool *Havnebadet Fisketorvet* (Vesterbro)—if you actually want to swim—to the sea baths at the coast that are just a short bus ride away. *Helgoland* off the newly-built promenade on Amager Beach breathes history, having opened in 1918 with a renovation in 2008. It makes a good option if you don't want too many kids around, as the water is quite deep. But the jewel in Copenhagen's waterscape is surely *Kastrup Søbad* (pictured), aka "The Snail". With an award-winning design making use of African azobe wood, this Amager Beach swimming spot offers magical nighttime illumination, gorgeous daytime views—and ample opportunities for jumping in.

• Various locations, see Index p. 64

Night **Counter Club**

It's surely a great society that embraces counterculture. State-financed, *Culture Box* has been quietly championing electronic music in Copenhagen for decades. Eschewing big names for more musically-minded lineups, the programme regularly consists of local and regional underground techno heroes. Fans of bottle service be warned: while the sound is pristine, the décor is minimal and the VIP section nonexistent. Come for a pregame drink at the club's bar, Cocktail Box, or prepare to wait in line with the throngs of loyal customers.

• Culture Box, Kronprinsessegade 54, Indre By, culture-box.com

Shop **Capital Style**

Danish fashion is booming, and Copenhagen is the place to shed money and acquire style. Every major city has a concept store—and the one here is *Storm*. Alongside wearables by cult labels like Céline, Moschino, Off-White and Raf Simons, plus local labels Tonsure and Astrid Andersen, it also stocks perfumes, printed matter, design objects and music. Head one block in any direction and be lured into *Stine Goya*, whose designs are fit for ladies who both lunch and lounge; *Ganni*, which does effortlessly feminine sun dresses and floral motifs as well as Parisian women do; *Wood Wood*, which stocks its own cool and classic streetwear, as well as pieces from peers and collaborators like Champion, Comme des Garçons and UnderCover, for men and women; and *Norse Projects*, dabbling in a sportswear aesthetic with an avant-garde perspective and an interest in Japanese specialty products. Stray a little further for the flagship store of *Henrik Vibskov*, Copenhagen's very well known conceptual designer (pictured). Practically next door is *OSV*, a secondhand store selling high-end pieces on commission, gently worn and sometimes new with tags. New stock comes in daily from brands like Acne, Wood Wood and Norse Projects as well as major international labels. You'll find understated Nordic refinement across the train tracks at *Armoire Officielle*. And a few blocks south, there's *Won Hundred*. Known for denim, it also riffs off traditional formalwear with a relaxed edge. Make these stores your markers, and happily wander into others dotted between.

• Indre By, various locations see Index p. 64

25

Jeppe Kjellberg
He is the frontman of WhoMadeWho, a Copenhagen-based trio formed in 2003 that plays party-hearty experimental pop. Jeppe's roots are in jazz music and he sometimes sings, such as on the 2012 Michael Mayer club-hit "Good Times". He has been living in Copenhagen since 1996

Jeppe Kjellberg, Musician

Tuned In

Since moving to the city from the small Danish island of Fyn, Jeppe has made himself part of the city's vibrant music scene. Here, he gives up some classified and unclassified spots of his town and explains why they're so special

Christianias Børneteater
Christiania

Sticks'n'Sushi
Vesterbro

Carlsberg Garden
Valby

Mother
Vesterbro

Copenhagen Street Food Market
Christianshavn

How's life in Copenhagen?

Life in Copenhagen is good in general. With WhoMadeWho we're in the studio recording our new album. We just released the compilation "Body Language" for the Berlin-based label Get Physical. Now we're making new music, as strongly as we can. Copenhagen is important for this. The perfect time is when spring comes. The city awakens after the long dark winter and the feeling is special.

How much is Copenhagen responsible for your creativity?

Very much. When you do music everything around you inspires you. In Denmark we make a lot of jokes about everything and are ironic about stuff. That's typical for Copenhagen and you'll find it in our music, too. When we play in the USA we always realise they don't understand this concept at all. But this ironic twist is an essential part of Copenhagen social life.

Without any irony: do you see Copenhagen as a modern cosmopolitan town?

Copenhagen likes to see itself as a metropolitan town. But it's also a cosy little place where only about one million people live. It's very local and everything is close by. In my opinion it's a bit like a little village—not like New York, London or Paris. Here you meet a lot of people you know on the street. All the time.

Is there something fresh and modern in Copenhagen right now?

I think there is a real creative and cultural blossoming. In music for a long time Danish acts just copied US or UK acts. But now you have artists like Lukas Graham at the top of the charts worldwide. Lukas is an example of good things evolving from this safe, welfare state capital. He grew up in Christiania, a nice alternative housing estate. It used to be a military area but the hippies took it over in 1971 and have lived there ever since. It is now maybe a cliché but I'd definitely recommend going and feeling the vibe of Christiania. Especially at the jam nights of *Christianias Børneteater* every Sunday—it's amazing there.

What do you most look forward to when you come back to the city?

The light here. Especially in the springtime. I really love it. I love to fly home in the evening when the sky gets all red.

Is there a great place to appreciate that light with a lovely view?

A nice place is the restaurant *Sticks'n'Sushi* on top of the Tivoli Hotel, where you have a view of the city and the Baltic Sea at the same time. They offer exquisite sushi and have a great selection of cocktails.

Whereabouts do you live in Copenhagen and why?

Valby, in the southwest of town. It's a quiet and cosy family district and it only takes me eight minutes to bike to the studio in Vesterbro. We have Valby Park, the largest park in town. Also the Carlsberg Brewery was founded here and it has the *Carlsberg Garden*, the private garden of the founder that's now open to the public. We have our studio in the formerly working-class area Vesterbro. Today it's a really popular area with restaurants, cafés and bars. If you're looking for a budget or gourmet dinner, the Meatpacking District in Vesterbro (Kødbyen) is perfect. We eat regularly at the Italian restaurant *Mother*, some say it's the best pizza in town. There's also the *Copenhagen Street Food Market*

The spectacular modernist extension to the Statens Museum for Kunst is linked to the older building by a "Sculpture Street"

JuicyBurger
Vesterbro

The Standard
Indre By

La Fontaine
Indre By

Assistens Kirkegård
Nørrebro

Vega
Vesterbro

that you need to visit on Papirøen (Paper Island). They have food from all over the world—it's in a big hall facing the waterfront.

Is there somewhere the band typically goes for lunch, or a drink after a tough recording session?

We often grab a gourmet burger at *JuicyBurger* in Kødbyen. And I recently had some amazing cocktails in this posh jazz-bar called *The Standard*—though the music wasn't so good. A great jazz-bar though is *La Fontaine*, that place is extremely charming and vibrant.

And what are other interesting districts of your town?

There's a multicultural area called Nørrebro in the northwest of town. Here you can take a drink in nice little trendy bars, often next door to dodgy pubs and kebab places. On Elmegade or Jægersborggade streets are many local design shops. The Sankt Hans Torv Square is the centre of the area and in summer you can easily lose track of time hanging out there in the sun. Also it's very close to the amazing cemetery *Assistens Kirkegård* where you'll find the tombstones of writers, poets and philosophers like Hans Christian Andersen and Søren Kierkegaard. Or local people chilling out doing yoga or reading. The atmosphere in Nørrebro is unique—it's a really creative place with the best nightlife.

And the best way to sample that nightlife?

Come and experience the Distortion Festival and you will be blown away. But my favourite place in Copenhagen to either play or listen to bands is the live club *Vega*. it has an amazing sound and vibe.

Royal Danish Theatre
Indre By

Café Dyrehaven
Vesterbro

Restaurant Geranium
Østerbro

Condesa
Indre By

Statens Museum for Kunst
Indre By

Henrik Vibskov
Indre By

Copenhagen is close to the sea. What waterfront places would you recommend?

To feel the water go to Christianshavn, in the middle of the city not far from Christiania. It's quartered by the Christianshavn Canal. You can find a lot of bars and restaurants there with a unique maritime atmosphere. The *Royal Danish Theatre* is also here and you can do a nice round trip by canal boat that takes you around the town from there or to places like Nyhavn, a 17th-century waterfront and canal which is good for a visit too.

As a musician: what are three albums you'd give someone who wants to discover Copenhagen through music?

First, "Polyester Skin" by Jacob Bellens. Bellens has a voice that evokes "hygge"—the typically Danish concept of cosiness—a feeling you'd find at a cool Vesterbro café like *Café Dyrehaven*. Second, "Liber" by The Minds of 99. This group sings in Danish with strong lyrics inspired by the greatest Danish poets. And "Niclas Knudsen Guitar Inferno" has the playfulness and open-mindedness you might experience at a club like Børneteatret in Christiania, where the free spirit still lives.

How would you describe the heartbeat of Copenhagen in one sentence?

"Hyggelig"—people are good at enjoying life in a very down-to-earth way here.

Can you name your most beloved restaurants?

Geranium has recently received its third Michelin star. Everything there is so carefully prepared and served with perfection. I went there with my girlfriend and tried the juice menu instead of wine. I never felt my senses stronger than that!

And somewhere for a more budget-conscious day?

The Mexican restaurant *Condesa* is amazing for tacos and more. It's a perfect starting point for going out too, since they have great cocktails.

What is your favourite public recreation area?

The park around the *Statens Museum for Kunst* (National Gallery). Honestly it's the combination of going to a great art museum that always has some amazing exhibitions and getting some fresh air with the kids in a cool playground.

And what about any shops for books and clothes?

In Krystalgade street and the Pisserenden area downtown you can find great clothing shops, like *Henrik Vibskov.*

What does Copenhagen offer that other cities don't?

Firstly, hygge. And intimacy. Then, many interesting things that are happening all the time within a very small area. And the city has an open-minded spirit that you only find in the best cities of the world.

Condesa turns into a party on Friday and Saturday nights, but don't forget to try the tacos

Nørrebro

Best of all Worlds

The smallest, most densely populated area in town is also where the cool initiatives, great bars and local shops are popping up. Multicultural, young and buzzing: Nørrebro is on the rise

Outdoors **Daning Out**

Taking up a healthy portion of Nørrebro is the famous cemetery *Assistens Kirkegård*, where visitors seek the graves of famous Danes such as storyteller Hans Christian Andersen and astronomer Niels Bohr. But locals tend to use the park in the cemetery's centre to meet with friends or throw blankets down on a sunny afternoon. With fewer graves in this section, it's not frowned upon—and the park is one of the prettiest in town. Only a few minutes away by bike is another spectacular outdoor space: *Superkilen* (pictured). What is essentially a large public park was created in 2012 as a collaboration between darling of the Danish architecture world Bjarke Ingels Group, local artist collective Superflex and German landscape architects Topotek1. A surreal sight from above, Superkilen consists of a red square devoted to physical activities, a green park whose rolling hills and vegetation make it perfect for recreational purposes, and a black market square where neighbours can get into the old school vibe by meeting around the fountain and tucking into a barbecue.
• Assistens Kirkegård, Kapelvej 4; Superkilen, Nørrebrogade 210

Shop **Defining Design**

Two contemporary Danish design gems stand on the charming neighbouring street Jægersborggade. In a quaint little pottery shop, local ceramicist *Inge Vincents* (pictured) displays her all-white designs on rustic wooden tables and shelves. With her delicate approach to the thin ceramic bowls, cups and vases, each item is handmade and unique. Just a few doors down is *Høj Copenhagen*, a haven for anyone with a head for interior design. The owners handpick pieces by small Nordic designers and sell art prints, pendant lamps and trays among other carefully curated stock.

• Nørrebro, various locations, see Index p. 64

Culture **Behind the Scenes**

Designs from upcoming local makers abound at *Værkstedet* ("the workshop"; pictured), a bright studio packed with prints, ceramics, wooden jewellery boxes, handmade ribbons and industrial design pieces. Initiated by an artist and an architecture student, here creators are welcomed to use the workshop at the back for different projects. All profits go to run the shop. *Blaa Galleri* is just a few doors down—a contemporary art space also focussing on emerging talents. There's a vernissage first Saturday of every month, and nine work spaces available for artists.

• Nørrebro, various locations, see Index p. 64

Shop **Nom de Plume**

After stints in Moscow, Paris, London and Oslo, Natalia Enge's Russian-Norwegian family settled in Copenhagen a couple of years ago. It must have been that globetrotting that helped her hone in on a gap in the Danish design market. She filled it accordingly with her store *Sirin*—the pen name of the equally international Vladimir Nabokov. The shop's eclectic homeware is flown in from all Scandinavia and the world, creating a concept store greater than the sum of its parts. Think fine French stationery, bespoke furniture and one-off prints by regional artists.

• Sirin, Ravnsborg Tværgade 7, sirincopenhagen.com

Food · Night **All Rounder**

On Nørrebrogade, *Gaarden & Gaden* is the kind of place where you'll just want to hang out all day. Luckily you won't have to move, since they serve brunch, lunch and dinner, not to mention tasty drinks and good vibes from various DJs when the sun sets. The menu offers natural wines, organic foods and black gold from The Coffee Collective. With its cosy interior, this café turned wine bar turned restaurant has quickly become a favourite among locals.

• Gaarden & Gaden, Nørrebrogade 88, gaaga.dk

Night **Talk it Up**

It's possible to have actual conversations despite the buzzing vibe at *The Barking Dog*—which allows for a somewhat older crowd. Punters are also drawn in by the quality creations whipped up by the bartenders. Long drinks are offered such as The Swede (lingonberry, vodka and dry tonic), alongside a comprehensive cocktail list. Look out for the Tree Hugger, containing vermouth from Piedmont, Danish gin, and organic agave supposedly created when the moon was aligned with Sankt Hans Gade street in Nørrebro.

• The Barking Dog, Sankt Hans Gade 19, thebarkingdog.dk

Food **Beer and Bites**

In an old locomotive factory on the tiny but happening street Guldbergsgade, dynamic craft brewery To Øl has its beer bar *Brus*. But the 750-square-metre mecca is not just for beer enthusiasts, with former Michelin chef Christian Gadient running the on-site restaurant *Spontan*. Meaning "spontaneous", the project represents his departure from the fancy restaurants of the capital to an industrial space and younger crowd. Fresh dishes adhere to seasonal availability—as well as the head chef's mood that day.

• Brus and Restaurant Spontan, Guldbergsgade 20, tapperietbrus.dk

Food | **Sky High Pizza**

Like pretty much every big hitter in Copenhagen kitchens, Christian Puglisi started out at Noma. But on leaving, the chef rewrote the menu at his restaurants Relæ and Manfreds. With these twin kitchens he shook up the fine dining scene by cutting prices and offering a casual environment—complete with paper napkins, fill-your-own-water and loud music. Then in 2014, he brought his fresh approach to the world of pizza with *Bæst* (pictured). Though born in Sicily, Puglisi's intention has never been to replicate "authentic" pizza—instead to create a local intepretation of the food. To that end he uses local grain for the dough, creates his own salamis in an on-site salumeria, and even produces his own bio-dynamic mozzarella, made from local milk in a micro-dairy upstairs and hand-stretched daily. Naturally the secret has got out and it can be hard to get a table. But sip a local craft beer or the house aperitivo at the bar and enjoy the wait. Puglisi's adjoining bakery *Mirabelle* provides heavenly pastries alongside brunches and dishes like home-made pasta. With practically the whole food chain represented on site, Puglisi seems to have constructed a whole world in his image: organic, locally sourced, seasonal—and downright delicious.

• Bæst, and Mirabelle, Guldbergsgade 29, Nørrebro, baest.dk, mirabelle-bakery.dk

Asger Juel Larsen, Fashion Designer

Unhurried Rebellion

Asger Juel Larsen

He's been subverting the norm with his eponymous label since knocking out his graduate collection in 2009. Plus he's also developed a seasonally fluid, unisex diffusion line A.J.L Madhouse. Danish-born, he studied in London before returning to the motherland. And his concrete knowledge of traditional British tailoring forms the foundation for his futuristic rave-meets-black metal designs

From just outside Copenhagen, Asger knows the lay of the land. Though working in the fashion industry, he's also immersed in disparate subcultures, meaning he knows the city's underground and high-end scenes well. Here, he shares secondhand stores, luxury boutiques, live music haunts and bars that don't do cocktails

Oysters and Grill
Nørrebro

Storm
Indre By

Henrik Vibskov
Indre By

Mads Nørgaard
Indre By

Wasteland
Indre By

Episode
Indre By

Limbo
Indre By

Lousiana Museum
Humlebæk

Jolene
Vesterbro

Assistens Kirkegård
Nørrebro

Where in Denmark are you from?
I grew up half an hour north of Copenhagen in a small town and moved to the city as fast as I could.

Was there a pivotal moment when you realised fashion was your calling?
It's been in the back of my mind since I was a child. Growing up I learned sewing, knitting, drawing and other basics from my mother, but mostly I was just living, not questioning the future too much.

You studied in London: what did it offer that Copenhagen didn't?
I wanted to study menswear design, so I thought the best was London. My five years there were some of the best in my life. The city swallows you and it's hard to leave again.

Is there something distinctly Danish about what you produce?
The long cold winter and the light summer do something with the way you think. I kind of bury myself in my work and when I get out on the other side, I have done a collection. What I make is a combination of my time in the UK and Denmark.

What does your label stand for?
It represents me, my youth, my life, my way of seeing things. It's unhurried rebellion.

Where do you go to grab a bite to eat?
Oysters and Grill has fantastic seafood.

Free time—where are you likely to be?
I'd be with be my girlfriend and friends hanging out at the lakes. One street Griffenfeldsgade is blossoming. It's worth checking out.

Where in Copenhagen can people get a real feel of the scene?
The Meatpacking District has clubs, bars and restaurants. It's a safe bet—no matter what you fancy, you'll find it. Refshaleøen is an old shipyard that now has events and festivals, especially during summer.

Where do the best-dressed Copenhageners shop?
I like *Storm*, *Henrik Vibskov*, and *Mads Nørgaard*. These stores have a good selection of established and new design. I also go to vintage stores around the Latin Quarter, especially *Wasteland* and *Episode*.

Any inspiring local artists?
Brynjolfur's electronic live set is incredible. Singer-songwriter Mø is great as well, and punk-rock band Iceage. The model and artist Sophus Ritto is also doing thought-provoking stuff in his gallery, *Limbo*.

And what galleries or spaces would you recommend?
You can pick one in the city, but I highly recommend the *Louisiana Museum*, a short train journey away.

After your successful Copenhagen Fashion Week, where did you party?
We had a big afterparty at *Jolene Bar* in the Meatpacking District.

What are some spots you take people new to Copenhagen?
I take them biking—you can managealotinaday.IliveinNørrebro—a vibrant and multicultural area. It's my preferred place, it has a local atmosphere and is very anti-stress. Christiania is charming; it still has its 1970s alternative vibe.

And where do you go to completely escape the creative scene?
I go to *Assistens Kirkegård* cemetery with my dog, Hank Lemmy Larsen. It's become a place where you can lie in the sun, picnic or stroll in between Hans Christian Andersen and Kierkegaard's graves. It feels sacred and calm and is good for recharging your batteries.

Brave Old World

A childhood in Christiania

Ella Forchhammer

Imagine a lake surrounded by trees. Walking along its shores you pass wooden houses in all shapes and sizes, beautiful gardens and quirky installations. You might come across people lounging in the sun, chatting on the street, biking to or from home and, probably, a few girls on horses. We're in the centre of Copenhagen, but this is no park. It's something more special than that. And it's my home.

This is Freetown Christiania—a place where people have come together in the hope of doing things a little differently. Founded on participation in all matters, from recycling and waste disposal to cultural events and political decisions, Christiania has been a—more or less—self-governing area since the original inhabitants took over a former military base in 1971.

Tourists might know it for "Pusher Street" with its famous hash market. Dealing and consuming cannabis are criminal offences in Denmark but here it is somewhat tolerated, with the term "Green Light District" being used in recent years. Nonetheless there are frequent police visits, and the area is often portrayed by the media as a nest of crime, unrest and social deterioration.

What growing up in Christiania was like is one of the questions I've been asked the most. Except, perhaps, "Excuse me, how do we get out of here?"—from visitors who strayed too far into our forest paths. But how a childhood there was different is difficult to measure, when you've never grown up anywhere else.

I was born in Christiania, literally, in my parents' living room. So were my two younger siblings. But I was quite old before I realised most friends had been born in hospitals. I'd assumed that was only if the mother or child was ill—since hospitals are for sick people. Christiania is in the middle of Copenhagen, so it's not from a lack of hospitals that many still choose to give birth at home. It's more for a sense of peace and security, being surrounded by loved ones rather than busy hospital staff and other birthing women. I celebrated my first few hours after leaving my mother's womb lying on my father's belly while he watched Denmark beat Uruguay 6–1 in the World Cup. It was a proud moment!

The images that spring to mind from childhood are of children playing in the sun, ice skating on the lake in winter, or roaming the area as far from prying eyes as possible—but always safe in the knowledge that help was near if needed. Christiania is a village—its physical boundaries are clearly defined. Within it, we could go wherever we wanted, as long as we watched out for each other and made it home by dinnertime—unless a neighbour was serving something more appealing. Many a call was made to work out which house was offering the best menu.

Christiania to me was comfort and security, with at least one parent always around. But my siblings and I were lucky—our parents provided a loving, secure home. Most families were like that, but some parents couldn't provide the stability and comfort a child needs. When I meet these children now, as adults, they tell me how neighbours took them in to give them the security they needed. In Christiania, they felt seen—part of a community. And when we meet today, we still feel part of the same extended family.

The area is a no-car zone—one of the reasons we were allowed to roam about as we pleased. There are numerous shops, workshops, cafés and galleries within the area, and maintenance work is taken care of by locals or closely connected people. This means Christiania is always alive, as opposed to neighbourhoods where everyone leaves for work in the morning, leaving the area deserted until the evening.

My parents met in Christiania—or in a bar nearby, I've never quite got the story straight—in the early 1980s. My mother had come to join her sisters—the four ladies are said to have had quite an impact on the place. My father too came to visit a sibling and ended up staying. He'd studied English and history in Dublin, after a short spell in engineering, but left his native Ireland aged 18. He worked his way around Europe and North America, stopping in at the famous Woodstock festival of 1969. He was a gardener in New York's Central Park—lodging with an Irish man whose son was fighting in Vietnam—jobbed on construction sites in London, and worked as a logger in the forests of Norway. In Christiania he was part of setting up a business restoring antique stoves and furniture from around Europe. On my way home from school, stopping by the workshop for a cup of tea—or to ask for money to buy ice cream—became a ritual.

My childhood home was always buzzing with life, guests coming around for dinner parties, barbecues or cups of tea. My father was a great lover of music and arranged tours for bands from Ireland, Scotland and the US. Often there'd be a band member or two staying in the living room, the porch turned into a rehearsing space.

In fact, there would often be someone staying at the house, or outside it. Once I came home to discover a tent pitched on the lawn, and two girls—possibly Swedish—having tea with my mother in the kitchen. She'd met them when she went to take out the rubbish, and offered them a place to put up their tent. It was probably from a sense that two girls should have somewhere safe to stay the night.

In the early 1990s, refugees fleeing the Balkans after the collapse of Yugoslavia were placed on an enormous ship in the harbour of Copenhagen. Whole families lived in tiny cabins with hardly any space to move. Many people in Christiania responded by offering their homes to refugee families when they went away on holidays. A family of four stayed in our house that summer, and I know my parents kept contact with them afterwards. The eldest daughter looked after us when my parents went out. I was a child and didn't spend much time considering global politics or war, but I often wonder what happened to them. Thinking back, I'm proud to have grown up in a community that didn't let fear of the unknown, or of unknown people, stop them from treating others with decency.

One of the things that sets Christiania apart is its relative newness. Most moved there specifically to be part of the community. Many came to avoid replicating the environment they grew up in, attracted to the idea that something could be created from scratch. They recreated themselves as cabaret singers, artists, rubbish collectors and activists in a place that—despite the disagreements that arise in a community of several hundred people—values each individual.

Whether their main reason for moving there is work, art, music, activism, anarchism, social change, architecture, nature—or simply a need to be left the heck alone—they all contribute to the uniqueness. Christiania is far more differentiated than the average village, while at the same time existing within the boundaries of a capital city.

Christiania has always been a hot topic, in the media as well as politically. That an area proclaiming itself to be self-governed should exist in the middle of Copenhagen has always been highly controversial. But excepting its earliest years, the community has always paid its taxes, water, electricity. Recently, a more formal arrangement was agreed. After years of negotiations with the Danish state, the Foundation for Freetown Christiania was set up to rent

the land and ensure it remains non-profit. Rather than being "squatters on military property", the foundation now owns some buildings and rents the rest.

But what seems to have been a persistent thorn in the side of government is Christiania's insistence on functioning as a collective. Decisions are made in general assemblies, and those negotiating with the government are a constantly changing group—rarely with any experience of official politics. To me, of course, that's part of what makes Christiania a unique and valuable place—exactly because it accents the communal as a way to individual growth.

The problem with Christiania becoming a "political object"—with acceptance of its existence depending on public and political goodwill—is the resulting polarisation. Examining the less savoury aspects of life in Christiania leads to conclusions like "obviously, it's a harmful environment, no children should have to live there" or "clearly, it's a nothing but a nest of social degenerates and criminals".

Of course, not every story about Christiania is rosy—like every other place it has its dark sides. Firstly, having to agree on all decisions can be tedious and infuriating. It takes constant practise and patience, especially when tempers rise. Not everyone has the same ideas of diplomacy and respect—it can take an awful lot of willpower to stop yourself from yelling at someone.

Secondly, the area attracts so many visitors it can seem more like a funfair than a community. On warm summer days, it's packed with people, quite a few high or drunk and many seemingly incapable of using a garbage bin. It must be a disappointment to see the place for the first time amid such chaos, as few tourists make it through the crowds to the quieter areas. It would be nice if more visitors would consider that people live and work here—and deserve a bit of privacy and respect. For instance, taking a picture through someone's living room window is not okay! Neither is leaving your garbage and empty bottles behind in someone's garden. Nonetheless, visitors are important—whether day trippers or those who stay on for a while. They're crucial for the area to remain open, alive and in a constant process of development.

That openness and liveliness provides the big city feeling, while growing up there gave me the closeness and security of a village. I grew up knowing that people are different, but that every person counts.

I have lived in Nørrebro, another part of Copenhagen, for three years now. I needed to focus on something other than Christiania politics for a while. I don't regret moving to the "other side of the fence" as we say in Christiania lingo. But I miss it every day! Living surrounded by trees and gardens, knowing your neighbours and being involved in projects that constantly challenge and develop your way of thinking is something I want to be part of again.

Ella Kathleen Forchhammer grew up in Christiania with her parents, Eugene and Eva, and her two younger siblings, Lukas and Niamh. Her brother's band Lukas Graham had an international number one with "7 Years"—a song about growing up in Christiania. Ella is currently completing an MA in English at the University of Copenhagen

Photos taken by and starring the Forchhammer family and friends in the early 1990s, in Mælkebøtten (the Dandelion), Christiania

Mikkel Sarbo
This former man of politics helms two teahouses, a Smørrebrød restaurant and the wildly popular Fleisch, a butcher and meat-centric restaurant. His experience in lobbying has helped him on a mission to keep Kødbyen cool

Mikkel Sarbo, Restaurateur

Cutting Edge

Mikkel Sarbo loves the Meatpacking District and he isn't afraid to say it. Here he fills us in on the history behind Copenhagen's hottest neighbourhood, why Vesterbro has broken all the rules and what you should be bringing back home

Torvehallen
Indre By

MadCooperativet
Indre By

Falsled Kro
Falsled

John's Hotdog Deli
Indre By

What area of the city do you live in, and what makes it special?

I live close to the Meatpacking District in Vesterbro. I love this place very much. It's changed a lot. You always have gentrification in cities—cheap areas attract creative people and when things get expensive and boring, they move on. But in Vesterbro something special happened: the people who came 20 years ago stayed. So it's become a small town within a town. We all know each other, we care for each other. And it's still a very creative, exciting place. People here chose not to buy expensive homes—instead of a car, they buy a cargo bike. This means they have more money to spend on, for example, food. So they go out a lot, making it possible to create nice concepts here. Of course if you want to move in now the prices are outrageous.

One of Fleisch's mission statements is to bring meat back to the Meatpacking District—did it ever leave?

It never left but the butchers here always sold directly to businesses. We wanted to make individual consumers part of the experience.

Some say your Meatpacking District is cooler than New York's...

I think that relates strongly to the fact that it's still a functioning meatpacking district. Here you see people who would normally not be in the city centre. We have a mayonnaise factory here, there used to be a liver pâté factory. You have actual industry next to the restaurants. There's a slaughterhouse where you can see the animals hanging and the butchers working with the meat. It's completely different from anywhere else in the city. And we wanted to conserve that. There are strict building laws now that don't allow you to change much, so it's difficult to make modern factories here. We wanted to make sure there were still butchers, still animals hanging, and we wanted to make it possible for normal people to come and buy a piece of meat. Also, it's under heritage protection, which forces us to be creative. You can't remove tiles, change colours. You have to adapt to the settings, so everyone has to invent new ways of doing things.

Something a traveling carnivore should keep in mind in Copenhagen?

We're famous for our pigs and export a huge amount of bacon. We have more pigs in Denmark than we have people.

You work with local farm suppliers—do you have favourite places in the countryside for a walk or a bite?

Dyrehaven is a great green area close to Copenhagen—easy by train from the central station or Nørreport, where you have *Torvehallerne* market, so you can bring nice food from there. At the central station we have *Mad Cooperativet* with great convenience food to go. For a romantic dinner, I'd recommend *Falsled Kro*, though it's far from Copenhagen (a two-hour drive).

For cheap and cheerful: your favourite hot dog stand in the city?

There is a traditional place with great homemade sausages called *John's Hotdog Deli*. We have a big tradition for these hot dog wagons —I think the food truck trend started with them! John started off ten years ago with a different approach. Hot dogs have been standardised but he makes his own sausages and creates different creative sauces. He's also got a small laboratory in the Meatpacking District where he develops new flavours. His cart is in the train

One of the stars of the Meatpacking District, Fiskebar offers fresh fish and seafood—as well as beautifully crafted desserts

station. From the outside it looks just like any other stand and he looks like any other hotdog salesman with a grey beard—but he puts a lot of love into it.

After the Noma-triggered Nordic food revolution and vegetable mania—what's the future of Danish eating?

I don't know how much influence we can attribute to Noma. I think a lot of foreign interest is linked to the Noma thing, but it's all related to other things. Denmark has been one of the countries where we spend less on food than anything else. Traditionally food has always been cheap and the discount sector is huge. Nevertheless, people have begun to use more money for food. Some grocery chains that focus on quality instead of the lowest price are winning market share, and have become very popular.

How has this affected Fleisch and the meat-eating philosophy?

That's for sure changing right now. People are keeping their meat but there are also many who would like to reduce the amount they eat. In our philosophy it's never about quantity, rather about the quality and the great taste of different kinds of meat. We are not 100% organic but we have quite a high standard for that. We very much like to know where the animals have been raised. There's also an educational angle in seeing the meat hanging and realising it comes from an animal. We'd like to be honest about that, so people know that when you eat meat it's a choice you make. We are not meat lovers in the sense that we want people to eat more meat. We want people to eat better, more consciously and be respectful of the animals in trying to use absolutely every part of them.

Kødbyens Fiskebar
Vesterbro

Spisehuset
Vesterbro

Nimb
Indre By

Ruby
Indre By

Salon 39
Frederiksberg

Anker Chokolade
Vesterbro

You're taking some friends on a tour—what's the plan?

I'd take them to *Kødbyens Fiskebar*. It's a fantastic place. It's actually by one of the original Noma guys, getting back to that question. He thought it was a shame you had to be a millionaire to eat great fish, so he opened this place. Another is *Spisehuset* in the Meatpacking District. They don't use signs—they think it's commercial. They want people to come because they appreciate the place or have heard about it. It reminds me of Berlin in the early 1990s, where you'd walk into a random courtyard and find a concert or a party.

You also own a popular "smørrebrød" stall in Tolvehallerne market—what's the magic behind this Danish food?

Smørrebrød goes in through the eyes—it's like visiting a donut shop. As opposed to the sandwich, it is very transparent. What you see is what you get. At our stand in the market we try to make them beautiful but functional. For example, many people put tomato because it looks good, but I only do that if the tomato makes sense with all the other ingredients on there.

Where do you go for a drink, to unwind after a long day of work?

One small place is *Nimb* in Tivoli. They make great drinks. There's a great cocktail culture forming, and in restaurants like Fiskebaren and Fleisch you have talented bar people making interesting things. They infuse things, go out and collect herbs... It's a way of playing with drink as with food. As for cocktail bars, *Ruby* is really nice and popular. Personally, I'm fond of *Salon 39*, where I have one of my first memories with my wife.

Where can we pick up some local delicacies to take back home?

It's not something we're known for, but we have some great chocolate here. A wonderful company is Friis Holms. There's also a great place close to the Meatpacking District called *Anker Chokolade* where you can pick some up.

You've also participated in city politics. Would you say you're a gastronomic activist?

Before I came in the Meatpacking District owners were fighting with the municipality about the development. They didn't want people peeing and partying in their industrial area; they also had to pay more taxes—everything was bad. I started to organise them better. We agreed this was how life was going to be and decided to make the best of it. And actually, many of those people find the district cool now. It's much more fun to be a part of this district than in a factory on the outskirts of the city. We've also worked for better conditions.

What's in the future of the Meatpacking District?

For us it's very important to try and keep as many of the old tenants as long as possible. We'd like the area not to develop much faster. If we make it too posh we'll lose this spirit. We have the world's biggest safe injection space opening. That means people who like everything to be polished might not come, but instead of trying to get the addicts to leave, we'll try to live with them. It's ok to see these kinds of people. We try to have some social control. If we get people with more resources to use the area, then we should reclaim the streets. We're trying to keep it special, and this is definitely going to be a part of that identity.

Spisehuset might be hard to find, but its décor, creative cuisine and wine list make it worth getting lost for

Side Streets

Jon Bjarni Hjartarson

Influenced by classic Scandinavian documentarists and explorations of urban space, Jon presents a side of Copenhagen distinct from its shiny surface

Sarah Britton
She studied design in Toronto before a stint working on an organic farm changed her life. After studying holistic nutrition, she launched her food blog "My New Roots" in 2007 to share her love for whole foods and a plant-based diet. She recently published a book under the same name and lives her healthy life in Copenhagen

Sarah Britton, Food blogger/Nutritionist

Green Scene

Copenhagen hasn't always been synonymous with food and good design. When Sarah Britton moved there, healthy food couldn't compete with "proper" Danish food like meat, potatoes and brown sauce. Seven years later, Sarah is happy to show us around a newly healthy city. Preferably by bicycle

Noma
Christianshavn

Morgenstedet
Christiania

Stedsans
Østerbro

Sarah, you were born in the US, grew up in Toronto and now live in Copenhagen. How does it compare?

Copenhagen is a little village compared to Toronto. And it's far more beautiful. You can wander around and enjoy just looking at the buildings. Toronto is not a very attractive city. I appreciate aesthetics a lot and like to be in a nice environment, so I much prefer being in Copenhagen. I also love the biking here. You have to have a death wish to ride a bike in Toronto, so it's nice to be in Copenhagen for that reason. I'm a major cyclist now.

The Danes are not only known for their bicycles, but also for their great food and design.

Oh yes, food is huge here and people really cook. That's another huge difference between North America and Denmark, they make dinner here every night. People just appreciate being at home and it becomes a real luxury to eat out. I think the Danes are healthier as a culture based on the fact that they cook. It is as simple as that. When you cook, you control the ingredients and are more connected to the food, the family and yourself.

What is Danish food like?

Traditional Danish food is all about meat and potatoes and brown sauce. And there is new Nordic cuisine which has been stirred up by Denmark and specifically Copenhagen and the restaurant *Noma*. It explores and celebrates the natural world here. Before the 1990s, when you went out for a nice meal, you were eating French food. So there has been an interesting shift. Foraged and wild food is now a worldwide phenomena.

You've been running your health food blog "My New Roots" for nine years now. Have you created some Danish dishes?

I did a couple, like a classical reinvention of "Koldskål", which means cold ball. It is like a mix of yoghurt, buttermilk and soured milk. It's a wet liquidy cream you put lemon and vanilla in, and eat with cookies and strawberries. You only have it for a couple of weeks of the year and then it's gone— it's delicious.

When you moved to Copenhagen, you worked at vegetarian restaurants. Would you recommend any?

Morgenstedet is cheap and cheerful, and the restaurant I go to most in Copenhagen. In the 1970s they only did breakfasts. Then it converted into a lunch and dinner restaurant but kept its name, which translates into "morning place". I worked there for three years, and that's where I learned how to cook.

What do you like to eat there for lunch?

There is a hot chef and a cold chef. The hot chef does a soup, rice with steamed vegetables, a sauce and something like a casserole. The cold chef does six to eight different salads, and I usually get the big salad. They know how to combine surprising things that you wouldn't normally think about—like lime zest in a coleslaw, or toasted quinoa with beets.

Are there any Danish foodies you admire?

Oh yes, Mette Helbak. She is a good friend and owns the organic rooftop restaurant *Stedsans* in the north of the city. It's spectacular and one of my favourite places to eat. They only use local ingredients, it's all organic and they are fostering a sense of community. Everyone sits

On an Østerbro rooftop, Stedsans offers the opportunity to join a community table and dine on farm-fresh cuisine

Höst
Indre By

Amass
Refshaleøen

Geist
Indre By

Manfreds
Nørrebro

Relæ
Nørrebro

Neighbourhood
Vesterbro

Naturpoteket
Christianshavn

on one table on the roof in a greenhouse. The food is delicious and super simple. There's no menu, you get what you're served. It depends on the night and what she's in the mood to make.

Where else do you like to go out for dinner?

It is very expensive in Copenhagen, so I don't go out much. However, *Höst* is really good—they do a vegetarian menu—as well as *Amass* which is located in an old industrial building. *Geist* is really cool, I've only been there once but it's totally bizarre. They are a forward-thinking place and really challenging. Some diners come away really inspired, while others don't really understand what they just ate. There's an open kitchen and you can see people cooking all the time. I also like *Manfreds* which is 100% organic and focuses on raw food. I've heard that *Relæ* is phenomenal.

So is it that difficult to find a cheap but good place to eat?

I went out to a pizza place recently called *Neighbourhood* in Vesterbro. They do organic pizza and vegan. It was pretty cheap—only 150 krones. That's a really good deal here. I always tell people: go to a food store and cook for yourself.

Are there any grocery stores you prefer?

Regular grocery stores carry almost everything in organic versions. There are some wonderful health food stores in the city I like. *Naturpoteket* is great, and there is *Helsam* in Frederiksberg which is big with groceries in the back. Just like *Helsemin*. Health food stores in

Helsam
Frederiksberg
Frederiksberg

Helsemin
Vesterbro

H. Skjalm P
Indre By

Hay
Indre By

Notre Dame
Indre By

Stilleben
Indre By

Torvehallerne
Indre By

Louisiana Museum of Modern Art
Humlebæk

Kongens Have
Indre By

Papirøen
Christianshavn

Botanical Garden
Indre By

Sofiebadet
Christianshavn

Amager Beach
Amager

Copenhagen are really different to US ones, because they just focus on dried goods and not produced stuff.

Which other stores do you like to go to in Copenhagen?

I really like the kitchen and interior store *H. Skjalm P. Hay* is really nice and *Notre Dame* has some good things. *Stilleben* is also a really nice interior store. I am addicted to plants so I find different plant shops around the city.

Does Danish design influence your way of working and living?

Coming from North America, we tend to be very busy with our décor. But I like the overall aesthetic here, the minimalism. I used to have everything out on the walls and now I appreciate good design and with nothing blocking it. When my mum walks into my apartment now she thinks it looks like a wasteland. I wouldn't call myself a minimalist but I have definitely been influenced.

What's your favourite area in Copenhagen?

I hang out in Christiania a lot because I am a nature person. Unfortunately, most people only walk down Pusher Street and turn around, without exploring the beautiful nature and residential area which is unbelievably special. Most parks in Copenhagen are busy. But in Christiania, there are all these secret little corners in the forest where there might be no-one around for hours.

If you have a visitor coming, what's on the must-see list?

I'd take them on a real tour through Christiania and then on a bike ride through every single neighbourhood. Recently, a friend and I made a good discovery—we were up on Jægersborggade and there are some good shops around there. It used to be very ghetto and now it's hipster land. I like Nørrebro and Vesterbro a lot. We'd also go to the central market *Torvehallerne*—it's a bit touristy but it's super Copenhagen, fancy and pretentious. So it's fun to visit. I like to go out to the *Louisiana Museum of Modern Art*—it's a beautiful gallery. We'd also go to the *Kongens Have* (King's Garden) if the weather is nice. *Papirøen* food market is also a great place for sunny days—look out for *Fala Fala*, which has amazing falafel salad. I love the *Botanical Garden*—its greenhouse is extremely helpful in winter when it's cold. I like to take my friends to a sauna—it's such a Nordic thing, and coming from Canada we're not used to nudity among men and women so it's always funny.

What's your favourite sauna?

Sofiebadet is the one. They have a beautiful hammam. On Monday nights, you can bring food and they set up a huge communal table in the centre of the sauna. Everyone has tea together and little snacks and takes turns going into the hammam. It's really cool—a nice thing to do as a family. And it's affordable.

When you have time off, what's the best get-away?

We like to go to Bon Ham. It is a bit of a journey, you have to take the ferry and bus but it's such an enchanted island. There's no internet, no phone, and we have this beautiful little cottage on the ocean with no one around. That inspires me a lot.

Where else do the Danes go to relax?

There is a huge beach called *Amager*. As soon as it's warm enough, people are at the beach. Lots of people have allotment gardens to visit.

Christian Puglisi brought creative cuisine into a laidback setting at Manfreds, famed for both veggie-consciousness and raw meat

What about the Danish concept of "hygge"?

Hygge is the overall goal of life for Danes. The only translation in English is cosy or cosiness. It can be a noun, an adjective or a verb. And it can be the reason for doing anything. Dinner with your parents, a bar, even a one-night stand—it can all be hygge. The Danes are very good at creating that cosy vibe, especially in winter. Danes burn more candles per person than anyone else in the world. They are such masters of aesthetics, because the feeling of cosiness and family is really important. I really like having that goal in mind like: how could this be cosier? That's what we're striving for all the time, the ultimate cosiness. It can be found anywhere.

Vesterbro

Meat and Greet

Traditionally home to the red light district and meat industry, Vesterbro is now capital of Copenhagen cool with a glut of eclectic cafés, trendy bars and happening restaurants

Night **Pack it Up, Pack it In**

Kødbyen, or the Meatpacking District, continues to function as an industrial area. But a heady development over past years has seen restaurants, bars and galleries mushroom, and the zone become a thriving weekend hotpot of craziness. For a relaxed vibe and local DJs spinning hip hop, the first stop is *Mesteren & Lærlingen* (pictured). Though just a tiny bar and dancefloor, it punches above its weight in good vibes. Electronic sounds, a crowded floor and a blend of DJs and live acts are the order of the day at *Jolene*. Vintage furniture is sprinkled in an industrial setting, with pornographic wall art to boot. And when early hours prompt the need for a true nightclub, day-time metal venue *KB18* becomes an underground techno haven, complete with the gritty digs to prove it. Indecisive party goers should rest easy—go outside onto the strip for a smoke and you'll see the magic of Kødbyen—with people from all the venues mingling together in one solid fun-loving community.

• Vesterbro, various locations, see Index p. 64

Culture **Accessible Art**

One of the first art spaces driving the makeover of the Meatpacking District was *Galleri Bo Bjerggaard* (pictured). In 2007 it moved to the industrial area, to a space big enough for two concurrent exhibitions, presenting fresh Danish and international art. The gallery's newer and more hands-on little sister is *Ekely*. It sells carefully curated art books, special editions, prints and sculptures amid a retro décor featuring wooden panels and walls that change colour to match the exhibition.

• Vesterbro, various locations, see Index p. 64

Night **Lab Libations**

In a three-storey former pharmacist's laboratory, *Lidkøb* has a beautiful interior complemented by a charming terrace decked with colourful light bulbs. A venture from the people behind Ruby—frequently cited as one of the world's best bars—Lidkøb manages to combine elegance with a down-to-earth quality. Choose between cocktails, bio-wine and home-brewed beer, and find a cosy corner to enjoy the drink with your company—or meet new friends at the communal tables outside.

• Lidkøb, Vesterbrogade 72B, lidkoeb.dk

Food **Piedi per Terra**

From the outside, there's nothing flashy about *Osteria 16*. But the tiny kitchen inside gives forth fantastic Italian cuisine. Seats are hemmed together in this unpretentious and down-to-earth place, making for a relaxed vibe. The menu is simple: enjoy eight antipasti and add dessert if you please. All ingredients are directly imported from Italy, with the carefully matched wine list including bottles from the owners' own vineyard in Piemonte. Popular with the locals, it's best to book ahead.

• Osteria 16, Haderslevgade 16, osteria16.dk

Food **Inside Out**

The classic Danish dish "smørrebrød" (open-faced sandwich) has had a makeover at *Øl & Brød*. Local brewery Mikkeller is behind the eatery, which occupies a beautiful space decorated with Danish design. Innovative, seasonal options might include veal brisket with pickled cabbage and pepper mayo, or potato with shrimps and crispy onion on rye bread. For dinner, Øl & Brød offers a three-course menu of Danish classics with a twist. Considering the landlord, try washing the smørrebrød down with one of Mikkeller's beers.

• Øl & Brød, Viktoriagade 6, ologbrod.com

Shop **Tiny Footprint**

It all started with Sundra's disappointment in the range of organic cosmetics available to her in Copenhagen. And it culminated here, in *Isangs*, a beautiful shop made of salvaged local furniture showcasing everything from vats of oils, infusions and "whipped butters" to old school razors. Pick up a bar of shampoo—which might have taken months to make—or share your dermal woes to result in a customised face mask created on the spot. Affordability is a part of the brand's identity, so you can do your skin an eco-conscious favour without breaking the bank.

• Isangs, Flensborggade 22, isangs.com

Food **Taco-Packing**

Noma's former pastry chef Rosio Sánchez has upped the Mexican game in Copenhagen. Under the alias *Hija de Sánchez*, she recently opened up two taco spots in the city—with the newest in the Meatpacking District. Providing a new angle on the classic snack, the higher price is justified by tortillas hand made daily from Oaxacan corn, and creatively adapted fillings. As a refreshing accompaniment, take some of homemade fermented pineapple drink "tepache". And watch out for guest chefs—including other Noma alumni—who contribute their own special twists.

• Hija de Sánchez, Slagterboderne 8, hijadesanchez.dk

Shop · Food · Night

Street Ahead

Same story the world over: dodgy street in red light district becomes haven of cool… It's certainly the case with Istedgade, now peppered with atmospheric cafés and funky boutiques. Wearing its Japanese influence on its sleeve, *Kyoto* (95) is a node for contemporary Danish fashion. This airy store features men's and women's wear, accessories and shoes from local designers like Han Kjøbenhavn, Le Fix, Ganni and Wood Wood. For smooth and minimal design, visit *DANSKMadeforRooms* (80) across the street. The two owners, sisters Ma-lou and Malene, handpick the best of contemporary Danish design from brands such as Menu, Frama and Eiermann—and you'll find both smaller interior pieces and larger furniture here. If you're looking to discover the Danish concept of hygge (cosiness) then *Bang & Jensen* (130; pictured) is a fast track. A breakfast buffet from 8–10:30am and a highly customisable menu, plus eclectic furniture and good looking clientele, make for a perfect Copenhagen café experience. Finally, *Malbeck* (61) is a wine bar that is tasteful yet relaxed—to end your stroll with a glass of South American red wine.

• Vesterbro, various locations, see p. 64

Maria Sattrup & Joachim Høst, Photographer & Artist

City Slickers

Maria Sattrup & Joachim Høst
Photographer Maria Sattrup is half of Sattrup & Høst, a cross-platform creative bureau whose latest project is provoking discussion on the dictatorship of smart devices. Former advertising film director Joachim Høst turned his back on winning honours at Cannes to reinvent himself as a painter, sculptor, photographer and documentary filmmaker. They've been together for more than 20 years

They call themselves real Copenhagen products. And when they leave their house they're in danger of falling directly into the world's cleanest harbour. Maria and Joachim explain the concept of "hygge" and what to look around Copenhagen for, if we manage to look up from our phones

Galleri LB
Indre By

Louisiana Museum
of Modern Art
Humlebæk

Statens Museum
for Kunst
Indre By

Fotografisk Center
Vesterbro

Kunstforeningen
Indre By

Galerie Asbæk
Indre By

V1 Gallery
Versterbro

In The Gallery
Indre By

Tango Grill
Indre By

Konya Kebab
Vesterbro

How much Copenhagen is in you and what makes the city special?

Maria: I was born in Copenhagen city centre and I lived here all my life. To me Copenhagen is its old buildings, canals and its relaxed atmosphere.

Joachim: I was born a little north of Copenhagen but I lived here all my life. My strongest memories come from exploring the city by bike in my youth and as a young, drunk party animal. When I am away, people can tell I'm from Copenhagen. I'm very, very proud of this. We've got this Danish word "hygge", it roughly means "cosiness"—a good, relaxed time. That's Copenhagen. Another thing we love is we have real seasons here. Our winter is very dark and depressing, but when spring comes, everything turns brighter and bluer and the city awakes with a collective "Yes, we've survived" uproar. And when the summer comes the city just goes berserk. It has an almost Mediterranean feel then.

Tell us about your latest ventures.

Maria: We just opened our photo exhibition "Digistracted" at *Galleri LB*. It's about how smartphones affect us; about how everyone is just looking at their screens and nobody is looking up anymore.

Joachim: We have three boys and were frustrated we always needed a rule about when they could look at their screens. The iPad, phone, Playstation... So I made a movie about it and during this process I found out I was the one with the problem—constantly checking my mails, Facebook, Instagram. My kids didn't know better. Our eldest is 14, just as old as Facebook. It's normal to them. So we started this project. So far the reactions have been overwhelming and we're taking the exhibition on tour. By the way, I just switched from a smartphone to a dumb phone from Punkt designed by one of my favourites, Jasper Morrison. I'm beginning a new life!

Does Copenhagen influence your work?

Maria: Of course. For me it is mainly the typical Copenhagen light that influences my work. I almost always do daylight photography, to try to capture that special Nordic light we have here.

Joachim: In general Copenhagen is very inspiring—if only because we have Tivoli amusement park right in the city. How awesome is it to have a roller coaster as a permanent part of the skyline? It tells you something about Copenhagen's playfulness—and of course that vibe sinks into our work.

What are your favourite galleries and museums?

Joachim: I just love the *Louisiana Museum of Modern Art*, half an hour outside Copenhagen on the coast of Øresund.

Maria: A beautiful location. Great architecture and a nice garden.

Joachim: Even their restaurant is great. They have all the big shows, new stuff and Danish classics.

Maria: Then you have the *Statens Museum for Kunst* (National Gallery), which used to be free but sadly is not anymore.

Joachim: And the *Fotografisk Center* which often has new shows. They have international exhibitions too, but their main focus is Danish fine art photographers.

Maria: Also the *GL Strand* art gallery over four floors in a nice old house.

Joachim: *Galerie Asbæk* on Bredgade, the Copenhagen gallery street. Asbæk was one of the first galleries to take photography very

Jagger
Vesterbro

LêLê
Vesterbro

Llama
Indre By

Christiania Falafel
Christiania

Royal Smushi Cafe
Indre By

The Market
Indre By

Lillians Smørrebrød
Indre By

Le Coin
Indre By

Cava Bar Playa
Indre By

Bar O
Indre By

Ruby
Indre By

Papirøen
Christianshavn

Torvehallerne
Indre By

GoBoat
Ørestad

Tårnet
Indre By

Botanical Garden
Indre By

Kongens Have
Indre By

seriously. It is a really old house with high ceilings, very beautiful.

Maria: And then *V1 Gallery*, with sculptures and paintings.

Joachim: Yeah they are the new boys in town. Very talented. And finally *In The Gallery*, named after the Dire Straits song, which mostly has photography.

That much culture makes you hungry. Any favourite restaurants?

Joachim: We love the *Tango Grill*, a tapas place. The Spanish chefs make the food right in front of you. A huge wine menu and affordable dishes, like the fantastic steak sandwich.

Maria: We love to hang out at kebab places. Our favourite is *Konya Kebab* on Istedgade.

Joachim: Yeah, our kids love it there. The guys working there are super cool and friendly. And it's extremely cheap.

Maria: Across the street, there is a typical American diner called *Jagger*.

Joachim: Good burgers and milkshakes—and you can even take cocktails to go in a plastic cup.

Maria: Then there is *LêLê*, a restaurant with Vietnamese street food. We also love *Llama*, a South American restaurant that turns into a bar/club after 10pm.

Joachim: And of course *Christiania Falafel*, the world's best falafel—at least according to stoned people.

Maria: *The Royal Smushi Café* is a nicely designed pit stop if you are going on a shopping spree in the high-end city centre shops. And as we love Asian food, we're often at *The Market*, a new and truly beautiful Asian fusion restaurant.

What is a typical Copenhagen dish?

Joachim: Smørrebrød, the open-faced sandwich on dark bread, is the typical Copenhagen dish. There are lots of places, although we mostly end up in *Lillians Smørrebrød* as it is directly in our building. Very cheap, fresh and tasty. We also often hang out at *Le Coin* for breakfast or lunch. It's in the shopping area, a nice place with the morning sun and local people.

And where for a drink or two?

Joachim: *Cava Bar Playa* on Ved Stranden is very nice—with a huge terrace and a vast selection of cava and wine. Then you have *Bar O*, owned by famous Copenhagen DJ Le Gammetoft. They play electronic music there and the crowd isn't too young, so you can actually go there being 45 and have a drink and dance. We also like *Ruby*, a great cocktail bar at the canal. Also, Nansensgade has a lot of bars, restaurants and typical Danish bodegas. Sometimes it's great to have a beer in those old fashioned bodegas and some even let you have a cigarette inside.

What is a must for Copenhagen visitors?

Joachim: Christiania! Definitely!

Maria: Yeah that's definitely a must. All these creative little houses—crazy architecture.

Joachim: In the 1970s the hippies squatted the old US Marine base and took it over. It is a city within the city. The problem these days is there are a lot of weed dealers, bringing crime and turf wars between gangs. It's a shame but it shouldn't keep you away.

Maria: Another must is *Papirøen* (Paper Island)—basically one big street food market. The ferry leaves in front of our house. *Torvehallerne* food market is also great.

Joachim: It's a bit more high-end than Papirøen. You can go there without being hungry and ten minutes later you'll sink your teeth

Romantic or bleak, depending on your mood: travelling Copenhagen's waterways provides another angle on the city

Royal Library Garden
Indre By

Ørstedsparken
Indre By

Kayak Republic
Indre By

Kayak Bar
Indre By

Funder Bibliotekshaven
Indre By

Black Diamond
Indre By

Harbour Bath Islands Brygge
Ørestad

into something absolutely delicious. Expensive but very nice.

Where to go for a romantic night?

Joachim: *GoBoat*. This is two guys renting out restored boats with a solar motor. You make a nice picnic basket and go on a trip through Copenhagen's canals. It is beautiful.

Maria: There is also a restaurant hidden in the tower of Christiansborg called *Tårnet*. It's very romantic having dinner there, overlooking the city.

And with the kids on a family day?

Joachim: Well, the sea and woods are never far away. If we're not in our little summer house outside Copenhagen, we love to take the kids on a stroll through the harbour. Or bike around the city. You have to rent a bike when you're in Copenhagen! It's amazing—somehow there's a new bridge over the canals every day.

Maria: And we like the many gardens. The *Botanical Garden*, *Kongens Have* (King's Garden), the *Royal Library Garden*, *Ørstedsparken*. There is a lot of green. Then at *Kayak Republic* you can rent a kayak to roam the canals. *Kayak Bar* is a bar by the water. They have frequent concerts going on.

Joachim: I'm getting romantic because we got married in the the Royal Library Garden. In there, you can hide for a coffee break at *Funder Bibliotekshaven*. And there's a new part worth checking out called the *Black Diamond*. They have amazing chairs to have a coffee and watch the harbour. Speaking of which, we also like to hang out at *Harbour Bath Islands Brygge* and go for a swim. Imagine, a harbour with clean water—where you can actually swim!

Editors' Picks

Northern Delights

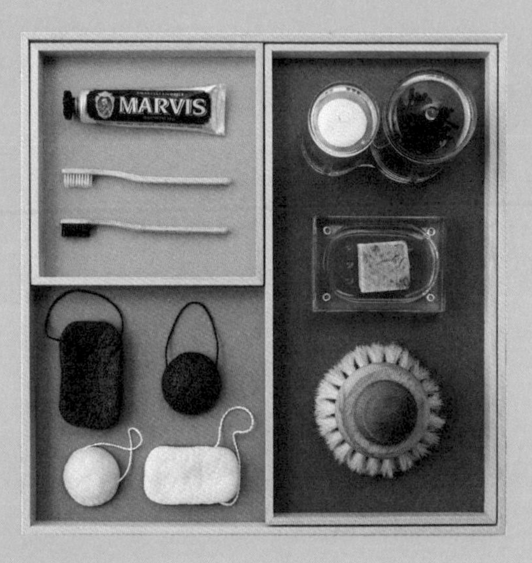

On a Platter

"Less is more"—the Scandi philosophy for all things aesthetic. In the spirit of simplification, make like the Danes and keep things tidy. These trays from the aptly named Nomess will come in handy.

• Display trays, Nomess, nomess.dk

Hot Dog

Born in 1934, Kay Bojesen's Dachshund has become a classic in the Nordic design archive. This rare early-edition specimen is available in teak at Secher gallery, where the little guy shares a home with hard-to-find pieces by other Scandinavian master craftsmen.

• Kay Bojesen Dachshund, secherfineart.com

Choc Full

A lesser-known Copenhagen speciality is chocolate. And former Michelin chef Mikkel Anker's take on it is avant-garde and delicious, as well as making the perfect edible souvenir to take home. Because smørrebrød doesn't travel well.

• Filled chocolates, Anker Chokolade, ankerchokolade.dk

Books

Nothing
• Janne Teller, 2011

Initially banned before becoming compulsory reading in Danish schools, this allegorical tale of a group of kids battling nihilism is hilarious, horrifying and unforgettable.

Smilla's Sense of Snow
• Peter Høeg, 1992

The obligatory Nordic-noir title on this list tells of a transplanted Greenlander investigating a little boy's death. Beneath the narrative lies an examination of Danish post-colonial society.

The Seducer's Diary
• Søren Kierkegaard, 1843

The narrator attempts to dominate a girl ten years his junior. An easier entry point into the work of the Danish giant and father of existentialism, available with a foreword by John Updike.

Films

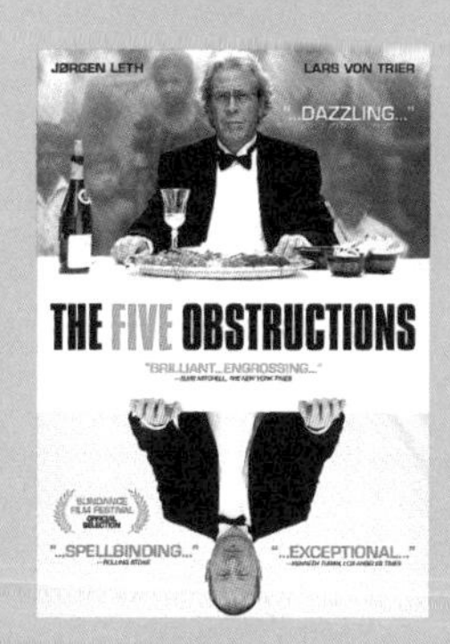

The Five Obstructions
• Lars von Trier, 2003

His traumatic masterpieces are well documented, but this fascinating documentary lays bare some of the workings of von Trier's filmmaking genius. In it he challenges his former teacher to remake a film five times with some crazy restrictions.

Italian for Beginners
• Lone Scherfig, 2000

The first Dogme film directed by a woman showed that an ethos which had spawned horrific views of the human condition could also be put to good use on a whimsical romantic comedy.

The Olsen Gang Sees Red
• 1976, Erik Balling

In their eighth film, the hapless criminals target a priceless Chinese vase. Blending slapstick and social satire, the hugely influential and beloved series was remade in both Norway and Sweden.

Music

Anti-Album
• The Raveonettes, 2016

This Danish institution pledged to their fans to put out one song a month throughout 2016. The end result "Anti-Album" is a musical puzzle of hauntingly beautiful songs about drugs, suicide and murder.

No Mythologies to Follow
• MØ, 2014

This rising star's debut studio album was quick to jump borders and climb charts, selling almost 1,500 copies in its first week in the UK. "NMTF" oozes youthful existentialism by way of no-nonsense lyrics, heavy synthwork and truckloads of energy.

Piramida
• Efterklang, 2012

Some people say Efterklang's sound is depressing—but listen closely for an underlying upbeatness. On "Piramida", Efterklang have reached their potential. The fusion of classical instruments and synths create a flying carpet of sound that sweeps you to the end of the fjord.

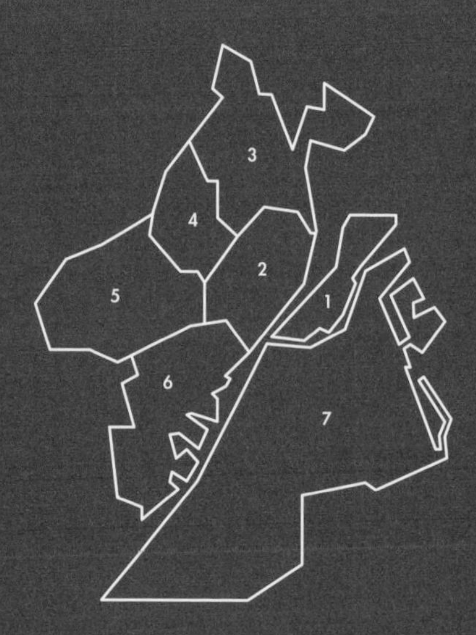

Districts

1 Christiania
& Christianshavn
2 Indre By
3 Østerbro
4 Nørrebro
5 Frederiksberg
6 Vesterbro
7 Amager

Index

Ⓒ Culture
Ⓕ Food
Ⓝ Night
Ⓞ Outdoors
Ⓢ Shop

Have all these locations at your fingertips with the LOST iN mobile app

1. Christianshavn

2. Indre By

3. Østerbro

4. Nørrebro

5. Frederiksberg

6. Vesterbro

DANSK Made for Rooms
Istedgade 80
→ p. 55 Ⓢ

Ekely
Istedgade 51c
bjerggaard.com
→ p. 53 Ⓒ

Fleisch
Slagterboderne 7
+45 61 68 14 19
fleisch.dk
→ p. 32 Ⓕ

Fotografisk Center
Staldgade 16
+45 33 93 09 96
photography.dk
→ p. 57 Ⓒ

Galleri Bo Bjerggaard
Flæsketorvet 85 A
+45 33 93 42 21
bjerggaard.com
→ p. 53 Ⓒ

Havnebadet Fisketorvet
Kalvebod Brygge 55
+45 30 89 04 70
→ p. 10 Ⓞ

Helsemin A/S
Vesterbrogade 6
+45 36 16 52 00
helsemin.dk
→ p. 49 Ⓢ

Hija de Sánchez
Slagterboderne 8
kodbyensdeli.dk
→ p. 54 Ⓕ

Isangs
Flensborggade 22
isangs.com
→ p. 56 Ⓢ

Jagger
Istedgade 62
jagger.dk
→ p. 58 Ⓕ

Jolene Bar
Flæsketorvet 81
→ p. 23, 52 Ⓝ

JuicyBurger
Flæsketorvet 44
+45 20 22 22 04
→ p. 15 Ⓕ

Kalvebod Bølge
+45 36 15 16 10
kajakhotellet.dk
→ p. 54 Ⓞ

KB18
Kødboderne 18
kb18.net
→ p. 52 Ⓝ

Kødbyens Fiskebar
Flæsketorvet 100
+45 32 15 56 56
fiskebaren.dk
→ p. 34 Ⓕ

Konya Kebab
Istedgade 47
+45 33 79 09 00
→ p. 57 Ⓕ

Kyoto
Istedgade 95
+45 33 31 66 36
kyoto.dk
→ p. 55 Ⓢ

Lidkøb
Vesterbrogade 72B
+45 33 11 20 10
lidkoeb.dk
→ p. 53 Ⓝ

Malbeck
Istedgade 61
+45 3331 1970
malbeck.dk
→ p. 55 Ⓝ

Mesteren & Lærlingen
Flæsketorvet 86
→ p. 52 Ⓝ

Mother
Høkerboderne 9
+45 22 27 58 98
mother.dk
→ p. 14 Ⓕ

Neighbourhood
Istedgade 27
+45 32 12 22 12
neighbourhood.dk
→ p. 49 Ⓕ

Nibble
Høkerboderne 16
+45 61 66 25 20
→ p. 55 Ⓢ

Øl & Brød
Viktoriagade 6
+45 33 31 44 22
ologbrod.dk
→ p. 54 Ⓕ

Osteria 16
Haderslevgade 16
+45 33 21 60 60
osteria16.dk
→ p. 53 Ⓕ

Restaurant LêLê
Vesterbrogade 40
+45 33 31 31 25
lele.dk
→ p. 58 Ⓕ

Spisehuset
Slagtehusgade 5C
+45 30 55 35 13
spisehuset.dk
→ p. 34 Ⓕ

Sticks'n'Sushi
Arni Magnussons Gade 2
+45 88 32 95 95
sushi.dk → p. 14 Ⓕ

V1 Gallery
Flæsketorvet 69–71
+45 33 31 03 21
v1gallery.com
→ p. 57 Ⓒ

Vega
Enghavevej 40
+45 33 25 70 11
vega.dk
→ p. 15 Ⓒ

7. Amager

Amager Strandpark
Islands Brygge 37
+45 33 66 33 19
amager-strand.dk
→ p. 50 Ⓞ

GoBoat
Islands Brygge 10 S
+45 40 26 10 25
goboat.dk
→ p. 59 Ⓞ

Kastrup Søbad
Amager Strandvej 301
+45 32 51 51 35
→ p. 10 Ⓞ

Harbour Bath Islands Brygge
Islands Brygge 7
+45 23 71 31 89
→ p. 10, 59 Ⓞ

Helgoland
Øresundsstien 11
+45 26 30 24 82
→ p. 10 Ⓞ

Other

Amass Restaurant
Refshalevej 153, Refshaleøen
+45 43 58 43 30
amassrestaurant.com
→ p. 49 Ⓕ

Bellevue Beach and Theatre
Klampenborg
bellevueteatret.dk
→ p. 9 ⒸⓄ

Carlsberg Garden
Valby Langgade 1, Valby
+45 33 27 10 20
visitcarlsberg.com
→ p. 14 Ⓞ

Hermitage Hunting Lodge
Lyngby
+45 33 92 70 87
slke.dk
→ p. 9 Ⓞ

Louisiana Museum of Modern Art
Gl Strandvej 13, Humlebæk
+45 49 19 07 19
louisiana.dk
→ p. 23, 50, 57 Ⓒ

Restaurant Falsled Kro
Assensvej 513, Falsled
+45 62 68 11 11
→ p. 32 Ⓕ

Available from LOST iN

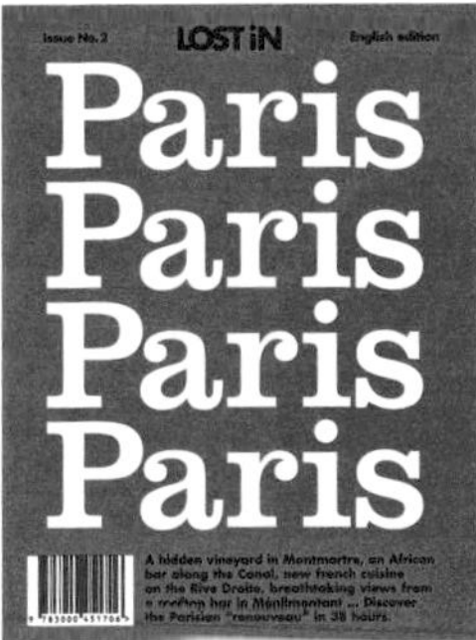

Next Issue: Warsaw

lostin.com

LAST SUPPER AT

NOMA

NOMA

NOMA

Story

Last Supper at Noma

Peter H. Fogtdal

I've always wanted to kill a thriller writer.
It's not because I'm envious, mind you. Envy is something other people suffer from. I just think it's unfair that 90% of the bestsellers in Denmark are crime fiction. During the last decade, we have become a country of cheerful executioners. If we can't kill people, we read about others who do. Yesterday the Danish Parliament passed a law that makes it illegal to write fiction unless you behead four of your characters, and three of them have to be women.

I find The Famous Thriller Writer at The Little Mermaid statue in the harbour of Copenhagen. It's a dark night with a sinister wind blowing in from Sweden. (Everything from Sweden is sinister). The Famous Thriller Writer has climbed up on the lap of the holiest Danish symbol. He rests his head against the Mermaid's naked shoulder and caresses her nipples with his crime-ridden fingers. Suddenly he produces a saw, cuts off her head, puts it in his briefcase and walks toward the Queen's palace.

I'm shocked but follow him through the night, past the Gefion Fountain, and down Amaliegade. My heart beats fast, but the darkness in Copenhagen isn't as scary as in other cities. It's a set of old, worn out pajamas, soft and comforting, a little too small over the chest.

The Famous Thriller Writer strolls over the square in front of the Royal Palace. All the dead kings follow him from their Danish Heaven, hovering over his briefcase with ancient breath. Centuries of drunken laughter can be heard in the wind. After all, Danes are the happiest people in the world, whether we're dead or not.

The Famous Thriller Writer continues towards Nyhavn and into the purple dawn. Slowly Copenhagen wakes up and puts on its bike helmet. Kids yawn with mouths full of cornflakes; teenage mothers put sunblock on their toddlers' foreheads. Unfortunately, I lose my man, so I run down Gothersgade and into Kgs. Have to see if he's hiding in the park. A blonde girl is counting her freckles on a bench. Two swans are devouring a piece of rye bread, but what the hell happened to The Famous Thriller Writer?

I find him again three hours later. He is on his way toward Noma, the best restaurant in the world. Outside there's a long line of tourists who hope to get a table before 2020. The Famous Thriller Writer still has the Mermaid's head with him, her nose sticking up from his briefcase. He gets the best table by the window and is joined by a man with a huge Adam's apple and a woman wearing Prada.

I stare with contempt at the three prose terrorists—at these mass murderers of language; cloak and dagger fascists as they are, with their cardboard characters and plastic plots, making a killing wherever they go. If they were true artists they would write haiku poetry in damp basements, but no, bestseller writers love restaurants where a bottle of wine costs the same as an apartment in Hong Kong.

I hide behind a Saab, while a waiter takes their order: radish pie, moss in pear wine, and Noma's specialty, steamed seaweed sprayed with urine from a Great Dane. (Noma only uses Nordic ingredients.) After dessert, the three get down to business. The Famous Thriller Writer opens his briefcase and shows the others the head of The Little Mermaid. The man with the Adam's apple produces the penis from Manneken Pis in Brussels. The woman in Prada holds up an arm from the Statue of Liberty but drops the torch on the table.

"We did it," they laugh and order brandies, but now I'm so full of rage I storm into the restaurant. On my way, I tell myself I'm doing this for the art of literature, for the 800-page epic novels in Mandarin that only are read by academics; for the postmodern memoirs from exiled authors in Syria, and last but not least, for the short story and poetry collections that cry themselves to sleep because nobody, absolute nobody wants to read them. And the reason? Some cruel, dyslectic God had the audacity of inventing thrillers and the Internet.

Then I shoot The Three Thriller Writers in the chest. But only metaphorically speaking. I'm a serious novelist after all.

Peter H. Fogtdal has written thirteen novels in Danish and four have been TINY best sellers. Three have been translated into French, two into Portuguese, and one into English ("The Tsar's Dwarf", 2008). Check out his award-winning blog, "Denmark for Dummies 2016"